smile
Awhile

Ethel "*Putter*" Weeks

Smile Awhile

By

Ethel "Putter" Weeks

© 2022

BWCE
PUBLICATIONS

Baptist World Cult Evangelism

PO Box 352

Jefferson, GA 30549-6711

www.bwce.org

All quotations of Scripture are taken from the Authorized King James Version.

Smile Awhile

© *2022 Baptist World Cult Evangelism*

PO Box 352 Jefferson, GA 30549-6711

Printed by Facing the Facts, Jefferson, GA

Cover Design by Addyman Design

Printed in the United States of America

ISBN: 978-0-9910115-5-1 (Paperback)

Dedication

Smile Awhile is dedicated to my parents, Joe and June Reed. Daddy and Mom are no longer with us, but while they were, they made sure all six of their kids knew they were loved, and they always made room in their hearts and home for many more who came through the door. Love and laughter filled our house; even during difficult times, there was always something to smile about and be thankful for; Mom made sure of it! They often told us, "We may not have much, but at least we have each other!"

Over the years, I have learned we really did have more than money could ever buy, or the mind could wish for; as always, Daddy and Mom were one hundred percent right, which makes me *smile awhile*!

Table of Contents

Smile Awhile

Smile awhile
And give your face a rest
Raise your hand to the One you love the best,
Then shake hands with those nearby,
And greet them with a smile.

Smile Awhile, do you remember singing this song in a church service? The congregation would sing this when they shook hands with those around them and greeted visitors before the sermon began. Just saying these words brings a smile to a person's face. (If you don't believe me, go ahead and say the words and see if you don't smile!) If anyone should have a smile on their face and enjoy life, it should be those who know the Lord and enjoy the blessings He has for His children.

Throughout the Bible, we can find Scriptures that teach about having a merry heart and joy in our lives. Some passages of Scripture have a bit of humor in them. For example, have you read something in the Bible and thought, "Now that is funny," or realized that the person commenting was "one of your people" by the way they responded to a situation with a humorous remark? Or perhaps if you are like me when reading an account in Scripture, I imagine what was happening in the minds of the people who heard what someone said or did, and I find humor in it.

Allow me to give you a few portions of Scripture that I find amusing.

In Ex 8:8-10, Pharaoh calls for Moses and asks him to inquire of his God and get rid of the frogs. Moses asks Pharaoh when he wants them gone, and Pharaoh answers **tomorrow**! Pharoah answered tomorrow, not now or as soon as possible, but tomorrow!

Pharaoh wanted one more night with the frogs!

In my "sanctified imagination," I can picture the conversation with Mrs. Pharaoh that night when he got home! I guess this comes under the "What were you thinking?" category in life.

Another account is in Exodus 32:21-24, Aaron's answer to Moses' question of why Aaron allowed the people to make a golden calf. First, Aaron tells Moses not to be angry with him;

after all, Moses knew how these people were, and they came to him (Aaron) and said to make them gods because no one knew where you (Moses) were! Then Aaron gives a rather humorous detail of how the golden calf appeared:

24 And I said unto them, Whosoever hath any gold, let them break it off. So they gave it me: then I cast it into the fire, and there came out this calf.

Seriously, this makes me laugh out loud. Picture the scene in your mind. After meeting God and getting the Ten Commandments, Moses comes down from the mountain and finds a golden calf and the people behaving wickedly. When Moses asked Aaron to explain what happened, he "passed the blame" onto Moses; after all, no one knew where Moses was, and then he explained that he threw the gold into the fire, and POOF out came a golden calf!

My next example is in Acts chapter 12, Herod, the king has killed James, the brother of John, and then he puts Peter in prison. Three things we are told:

1. The Church is praying without ceasing for Peter.

2. Peter is bound with chains between two soldiers.

3. The doors of the prison were also guarded.

Then in verse seven, Peter is delivered by an angel of the Lord and led out of prison, and in Ac 12:12, we read that Peter came to the house of Mary, the mother of John, whose surname was Mark, where many had gathered together to pray for him.

Peter makes his way to the house of Mary, where many are praying for him. When he knocks on the door, a young girl named Rhoda comes to the door, recognizing his voice; instead of letting him in, she runs to the "prayer room" to tell them that Peter is here; however, Peter is still standing on the porch!

In my mind's eye, I see Peter standing outside, wondering what just happened and calling out her name, "Rhoda, oh Rhoda, yes, it is me, Peter, open the door!" "Rhoda, oh Rhoda! Please open the door!" If Peter could have seen what was happening in the "prayer room," he would have been even more perplexed!

Those in the "prayer room" did not believe her, and we read that she constantly affirms that it is Peter, but they think it is Peter's angel (a messenger or divine angel with a message about or from Peter).

Meanwhile, out on the porch, Peter continued knocking: and when they finally opened the door and saw him, they were **astonished**.

First, Rhoda, the young girl, lets him stand on the porch, and then the others don't believe her, and when they finally see Peter, they are astonished!

I am not sure which I find more humorous, Rhoda not letting Peter in or the "prayer warriors" not believing Peter is outside and their prayers were answered.

But to be honest, I must admit, I often react like the "prayer warriors." I pray for a good outcome for a situation but am astonished when the Lord brings it to pass! But I guess some things never change.

Numbers twenty-two is another biblical account that I find funny, tragic, but funny. It is the account of Balaam, the spokesperson of God, who is out of God's will, and how the Lord uses a donkey to get his attention. First, Balaam gets mad at the donkey and hits it; then, the donkey begins to talk to him! Yes, he talks to him, and Balaam answers him! But Balaam was so bent on doing things his way and out of God's will that he didn't realize he was having a two-way conversation with an animal.

The last one I want to mention is the account of Elijah and the prophets of Baal at Mt Carmel in 1Kings 18:17-40; read for yourself how Elijah answers the prophets of Baal and catch the humor in his voice, as he uses humor to make his points.

Our Christian life is to be enjoyed, not endured. Therefore, it is okay to enjoy life and even laugh in crazy, difficult, and unfortunate situations. Laughter is essential to our spiritual well-being.

"As soap is to the body, so laughter is to the soul."
(Jewish Proverb)

Think about the above statement for a moment. What soap does for the body, laughter does for the soul. Soap cleans and renews the body; laughter does this to the soul! Therefore, as we live out our life in Christ, we are to live a joyous life, as we learn from the following verses:

Psalms 16:11 Thou wilt shew me the path of life: in thy presence is fulness of joy; at thy right hand there are pleasures for evermore.

Psalms 4:7 Thou hast put gladness in my heart, more than in the time that their corn and their wine increased.

The book of Proverbs reminds us of the benefits of having a merry heart:

Pr 15:13 A merry heart maketh a cheerful countenance: but by sorrow of the heart the spirit is broken.

Pr 15:15 All the days of the afflicted are evil: but he that is of a merry heart hath a continual feast.

Pr 17:22 A merry heart doeth good like a medicine: but a broken spirit drieth the bones.

And, of course, we all know the familiar verse in Ecclesiastes 3:4: A time to weep, and a time to laugh; a time to mourn, and a time to dance.

Lord Byron said: *"Always laugh when you can. It is cheap medicine."* (I wonder if Lord Byron knew Pr 17:22.)

Laughter is good for our health and our soul. We often laugh over: silly things, absolutely dumb things, and things that only we think are funny, and how often have we laughed during inappropriate times? Have you ever tried to suppress a laugh during a church service? The longer you try not to laugh, the funnier "it" seems!

Here are a few quotes about laughter and humor; some are thought-provoking, and others are just funny:

A good laugh is sunshine in the house. William Thackeray

A smile starts on the lips, a grin spreads to the eyes, a chuckle comes from the belly; but a good laugh bursts forth from the soul, overflows, and bubbles all around. Carolyn Birmingham

Laughter has no foreign accent. Paul Lowney

Whatever your heartache may be, laughing helps you forget it for a few seconds. Red Skelton

The human race has one really effective weapon, and that is laughter. Mark Twain

Trouble knocked at the door, but, hearing laughter, hurried away. Benjamin Franklin

Wrinkles should merely indicate where the smiles have been. Mark Twain

You don't stop laughing because you grow old. You grow old because you stop laughing. Michael Pritchard

It is better to laugh about your problems than to cry about them. Jewish Proverb

A keen sense of humor helps us to overlook the unbecoming, understand the unconventional, tolerate the unpleasant, overcome the unexpected, and outlast the unbearable.
Billy Graham

There are four areas where laughter will benefit us throughout our lives that you will read about in the pages of this book. The first one is being able to laugh at ourselves, the second one is to laugh during difficult times, the third is to learn to laugh and see the joy in getting older, and the fourth is not about us laughing, but when God laughs.

Each topic is an experience I have gone through during my walk with the Lord. Each step of the way, He has always been beside me, and through it all, He has given me a daily dose of His best medicine, a merry heart.

As you read this book, I trust you will be encouraged and helped in your everyday situations and enjoy a few good laughs.

Dear Lord Jesus,
May those who read this book,
for a little while,
forget their troubles and smile awhile.

Laughing At Yourself

"You grow up the day you have your first real laugh . . .at yourself."

Ethel Barrymore

Over the years, I have often had occasions to do just that, laugh at myself! Of course, most of these were situations that just happened; however, I must admit, quite a few would fall under the title of *absolutely dumb* and *what was I thinking* category!

There was one night, or I should say early morning, when our doorbell rang at three AM. I still laugh at myself whenever I think of this scared young wife and mother frozen with imaginary fear.

First, allow me to "set the stage" for my situation. I am easily frightened. I grew up the third child in a family of six, and for some reason, my siblings thought it funny to hide from me and pop out of closets, corners, and under tables to scare me; it worked every time, much to their laughter. They did not know they were setting me up for a lifetime of being easily frightened.

Yes, I still frighten easily, only now my kids and grandkids are the ones popping out of closets, corners, and from under tables or behind doors to scare me, and it works, much to their laughter!

Our one grandson, Zane, loves to hide in corners or sneak up on me and scream to see me freak out! He finds my reactions very amusing and will laugh until he doubles over. He gets this uncanny ability from his mother, who does the same, but I digress back to my story.

My husband worked nights; he would leave the house at 11 PM and return around 7 AM the following day. It took me about a year to get used to this schedule and to learn to sleep without him in the house. My mother-in-law lived with us then, and we had our two oldest girls, who were four and five years old. Fortunately, my mother-in-law and the girls slept through the night very soundly.

One early morning our doorbell went off; now, this was no ordinary doorbell; it played a beautiful chime; each chime was four notes, and it would play them twice, eight times for one ring!

Imagine now, the house is quiet, all are sleeping, and at three AM, the doorbell goes off; I get up and run to the door; after all, I don't want the kids to wake up at three AM! As I got to the door, I looked through the window and saw a stranger, a man! Then as I begin to go for the doorknob, I see his car pulled over in front of our house, but it is still running!

Realizing we girls are all alone, and it is three AM, I decided to ask a simple question: **Who is it**? The minute I opened my mouth, fear struck me, and I could not speak above a whisper, and my knees buckled, and I had to grab the chair near the door before I hit the ground. So there I stood, bent over the back of the chair, knees buckled, hanging onto the chair to stay upright and saying, ever so quietly," Whoo . . . whoo . . .whoo!

The man rings the doorbell again, **another eight times.** I thought for sure he would wake the girls, and when they saw me in the state I was in, they would naturally be petrified! Then as I managed to look out the window, I saw another man running toward him, and they both took off and drove away.

You would think I would have composed myself, but fear gripped me even more, for I knew they were up to no good and had just "cased" the house, and I figured they would be back to break in! So, what did I do next?

Well, most rationally minded women would have called 911, but nothing was rational about my thinking at that moment!

I managed to wobble into our girls' room, closed the door, and pulled their dresser up against the door! I figured this would give us time to jump out the window if they came back and broke into the house! About fifteen minutes later, as I sat on the edge of one of their beds, I saw blue lights flashing! It was police lights, so I got brave enough to move the dresser back, open the door, go to the kitchen, and look out a window! My girls never woke up! (Neither did my mother-in-law!)

I felt terrible when I found out what had happened. We lived in the country, and a man had fallen asleep while driving and his car went up over a bank and wrecked his car. The man at my door saw it happen, and since there was a car in our driveway, and I had the outside lights on and a night light on in every room in the house, he assumed someone was home, so he rang our doorbell in hopes that someone would call 911. (This was before everyone owned a cell phone.)

Fortunately, the man was not hurt, but I still felt terrible that I was so scared I could not even talk, let alone dial 911, but I realized I finally knew the answer to a question that had bothered me for years. I had often thought: what would I do if I were scared or felt threatened? I found out that night what I would do! Absolutely nothing!

And today, even though I still laugh at myself when I think about this night, I think I missed a chance to meet an angel, for the only verse I could think of that night to help me in my moment of panic was: Hebrews 13:2 "Be not forgetful to entertain strangers: for thereby some have entertained angels unawares."

Fast forward 30+ years later, I found myself in another crazy situation! A self-induced situation that I can only laugh at myself and ask, "What was I thinking?"

One afternoon my daughter, Mary Beth, and I were out shopping, and when we were finished, she dropped me off at our house and went to the grocery store to pick up some things and would return home in a few minutes.

As she drove out of the driveway, I went to unlock the kitchen door, but I realized I did not have my house keys with me, but it was not a problem, she would be back in a few minutes, so I would wait for her to return. (This also happened before we had cell phones!)

I walked around the house to our screened-in porch to sit down until she returned, but once on the porch, I saw the unlocked kitchen window right above the picnic table! (Some of you are already ahead of me, aren't you?)

I got up on the table, opened the window, and looked around; praise the Lord, there were no dishes in the sink! So, I say to myself, "Putter, you got this; after all, you climbed the ropes in gym class; how hard can it be to climb in through a window?"

I forgot this was not a regular-size window; it was about half the size of a standard window, and the most important thing I forgot was that I wasn't as young as I was in gym class!

It was not hard at all . . . for the first leg to go through, then just a little twist here and there, and my upper body made it through! I was beginning to feel like the man who fell out of a 20-story building; as he fell past the 10th floor, he was heard saying, "So far, so good!"

As I brought my right leg up to get it in the window, I got the WORSE CRAMP I have ever had! On a scale of 1 to 20, it was at least a 30! I could not bring my leg down, nor could I bring it up, nor could I bring my upper body out of the window! I was stuck in a window! I dangled half in, half out, with a crippling pain in my hip.

In my moment of despair, I realized I could have some fun with this when Mary Beth came back! Suddenly the pain did not seem so excruciating as I anticipated the look on her face as she walked into the kitchen and saw her mother dangling from the kitchen window!

I would be the first thing she saw when she walked through the back door. So, when Mary Beth walked in, I thought I could holler something like, "hands up!" I was beginning to like the idea of being stuck, but I was praying that she would hurry back to the house before I passed out with pain from the hip cramp and missed all the fun!

As she unlocked the door and walked in, she saw me first, and her reaction was priceless; she was scared, shocked, and amused all at once. As she stood there, laughing, I finally had to say, "Stop laughing and help me get out of this window!"

Believe me, when I think of this now, I am so glad Facebook wasn't around, I know Mary Beth, and she would have had to make a video first and post it on Facebook; I would forever be known as the "Old Woman stuck in a Window!" I am sure that video would have had at least five shares from all my other kids and a million likes! (And no, Mary Beth, we will not do a "do-over" for you to take a video today!)

Yes, being able to laugh at yourself is always good, especially when there is nothing we can do about a situation but laugh, and recently I found myself in such a situation.

I had to laugh at myself over a great accomplishment and goal I had reached, but in this laughter, I also learned a very good lesson and lived out the meaning of "pride goeth before destruction!" Pr 16:18.

I had been on a healthy eating plan for about a year, producing a much-needed weight reduction. Yes, the diet plan worked, and the best part was a new wardrobe; however, I forgot to replace one essential item of clothing.

I do not like to wear pantyhose. I never could find a pair that fit comfortably. To get a size for a good fit in the thighs, the foot was too large, and the waist was always too tight, and with my short legs, the legs were always too long and would wrinkle up!

So, for years I have worn thigh-highs. A few months after my diet, I put on a pair of them and went to the mall to walk around with my hubby. Once inside, I walked around the Mall, and he walked to his favorite store, the iPhone store!

As I walked around, I felt rather good about myself as I saw my reflections in the windows; okay, to be honest, I was feeling pretty proud of how I looked! However, as I walked on the second floor, I felt something odd on my leg and realized my thigh-high stocking was slipping down my leg. I forgot to replace my old thigh-highs with new, smaller ones! The elastic in these was stretched out, and they did not stay up. The longer I walked, the faster they slipped down!

I managed to pull it discreetly up and went on my merry way for about 50 more steps. Then I realized the other leg was now slipping down! I was too far from the bathroom to go and take them off, but I could see the exit door; I called Dave and told him to meet me at the car because I was experiencing a "wardrobe malfunction."

I now resembled Quasimodo, the Hunchback from Notre Dame, as I walked bent over, trying to hold my stockings up, but by the time I got to the door, I was wearing knee-highs. I knew I could not walk through a parking lot doing my Quasimodo imitation. I would surely trip over my own two feet or run into parked cars!

As the hose slipped further down, I realized: "it is what it is," so I stood up straight and walked to the car! I got to the car just in time to take off my ankle highs!

So, ladies, learn to laugh at yourself; it really is the best medicine, especially if you have a wardrobe malfunction!

I hope you have had a good laugh over a few of my "what were you thinking" moments. There were so many other laughable moments during my life; like the time I wanted to dry my little girl's shoes and thought the oven would be an excellent place to dry them quickly; if you ever try that, keep the temperature very low, don't walk away from the oven and have 911 on speed dial for the fire department and the time I forgot I had chicken in the oven, let's say having 911 on speed dial, was a big help and so was the strange man who ran through my house to make sure there were no other people in the house! And the most recent one of how I thought I would save us money when the Pandemic hit by making reusable masks! The names: Princess Lea from Star Wars and Daffy Duck came to mind when I modeled them for my kids!

If you find it hard to laugh at yourself, remember this quote from Fred Allen: "It is bad to suppress laughter, because it goes back down and spreads to your hips!"

Dear Lord Jesus,
May we be serious but not take ourselves so seriously that we forget to enjoy this life You gave us with joy, and may we always be able to laugh at ourselves and learn to smile awhile.

Laughter During Situations That Are Out Of Our Control

How many of you have seen the movie *Steel Magnolias*? One scene in this movie that is a perfect example of laughter in the face of situations that are out of our control is the funereal scene. When M'Lynn and her girlfriends are leaving the cemetery, she finally breaks down and cries, and then one of her friends says something that makes them all laugh. Yes, they laugh during a difficult situation they have no control over! This scene reminds me of the verse Ec 3:4 "A time to weep, and a time to laugh."

A time to weep and a time to laugh; have you ever been in a situation where you did just that, first you cried, then before you knew it, you found yourself laughing? I did, and it was in the same setting as the scene from *Steel Magnolias!* A time when I felt just like M'Lynn and went from weeping to laughing.

My siblings and I had a *Steel Magnolias* moment at my mother's funeral. Bear with me briefly as I introduce you to my mother. Anyone who has ever met my kids has met my mother, June, for each of them is like Mom in one way or another and sometimes two, for which I am most thankful because, in that respect, my mother lives on through them.

Mom was a friend to all and had a heart for those who needed help. She always found someone who needed a little love in their life; she had six children but was a mother to many more. You have all heard the saying: "It takes a village." Mom was that village for many of our friends when we grew up. She always said, "There is always room for one more!"

She was the original Energizer Bunny; the woman could not sit still. This phrase described Mom: *if you can't change the world, change your world*! That was Mom, and she changed her world with a paintbrush or a cleaning brush! If you stood still long enough, she put you to work or painted over you!

She decided she would like a larger kitchen when she was expecting me. The house we lived in had a small room off the kitchen, and she wanted the wall knocked down to have a larger kitchen. My Dad kept telling her it could not be done, but that did not stop Mom. One day, while he was at work, she decided to show him it could be done! Imagine his surprise when he got home from work and found her sawing through the support beam!

After this episode, Daddy always made sure he was completely clear with his explanations to Mom as to why something could not be done; however, she made it easy for us girls to get our husbands to do things around the house, for all we had to say was, "Oh, don't worry about it Honey, I'll just call Mom!"

She was also known as the woman whose house was so clean that you could eat off her floors! And you really could. She cleaned like most women spring cleaned every week and on snow days during the school year.

Can you imagine the joy of a child to hear school is canceled because of snow and the anticipation of playing in the snow and snowball fights and snowman building and sledding down a hill only to have your mother open your bedroom door with a bucket, mop, and dust cloth and with a smile on her face telling you and your sister that this is a great day to clean your bedroom!

However, when we were smaller, she made cleaning fun for us kids. Another house we lived in had a large living room with wooden floors. She would get on her hands and knees and wax the floor with a paste wax! Then, she would give each of us kids old towels to slide on the floor until it shined! We never realized she had put us to work; we thought we were having fun!

She not only cleaned all the time but moved the furniture around every time she cleaned. As a result, there never were any wear spots on the carpet or floors because she moved the furniture too frequently to make any marks! She was also known to change rooms often; therefore, our house never looked the same from one week to the next.

Once she switched out bedrooms, no big problem, except for the time my Dad was working 2nd shift and came home in the wee hours of the morning, crawled into bed, put his arm around Mom, and kissed her on the cheek, much to his, and my brother's surprise!

As he went to work the next day, Dad told Mom that when he came that night, he would appreciate it if she put the rooms back the way they were; somehow, Daddy and my brother never did see the humor in her changing rooms! However, that did not prevent her from moving furniture around; she continued up to the day of her funeral!

Mom always had one request for when she passed away; it was simple; if people did not come to see her when she was living, she did not want them to see her when she was all laid out in a coffin. She just wanted her family and close friends there. So, we honored that, and at her funeral were her six kids and their spouses, grandchildren, and a few of her friends.

We had a service at the funeral home. My sister's Pastor, who only met Mom while she was bedridden a few months before her death, said sweet words about her and gave a short comforting message from Ps 23. And then he asked her kids and grandkids to say what they wanted to about Mom, and afterward; we would make a circle, hold hands, and those who wanted to, could pray.

To do this, we had to move all the chairs out of the way to form a circle; of course, it was a very emotional moment, we girls and grandkids were crying, and my brothers were holding back their tears. Then, as we moved and rearranged the chairs, my younger brother started laughing, looked at us, and said, "She's back!"

At that moment, a moment that we had no control over, a moment where we were weeping, suddenly turned to laughter! It was as if Mom had pre-arranged the moving of chairs to remind us that life goes on.

Yes, we wept over her passing, but then we laughed, just like Mom would have wanted us to do!

Let me stop here a minute and say that I realize the death of a loved one is never an easy road to walk. We have all, undoubtedly, experienced the loss of a loved one, and even though the hurt never goes away, we somehow go on. We find our own place, not in their shadow, for we are not them. We carve out our own path. It may be something completely different from what we were used to, but there is a path for us; we need to be patient and allow the Lord to lead us to find our new normal.

I want to offer some advice to those who have friends who have lost a loved one; please allow them to talk about their loved ones who have passed. So many times, after each of my parents, passed away, I wanted to talk about them, their life, and their death, but whenever I did, my friends would change the subject.

I was confused and hurt by their actions, then one day, I found out why people do that. A Psychologist explained this on a TV program I just happened to be watching. This is a very real occurrence at the death of a friend's loved one.

People are frightened that if they talk about your loved one's death, it will happen to them. For example, talking about my parents' death to my friends made them afraid their parents or loved ones would pass away, so they changed the subject!

So, if you know someone grieving over a loved one, please lend them a listening ear and listen to their stories, it is good for them, and you will be glad you helped them over their grief.

I said all that to say this: after I learned this about the grieving process, I was determined to remember it to help others during their grief like I longed to be helped over my grief over my parents' death. Little did I know that this desire to help others in their grieving process would take me down a road I had no control over, but I was able to be a blessing to someone in need of an understanding ear during their grief over the loss of their. . . pet!

Yes, I said pet; those who know me know I am not an animal lover. I apologize to all of you who are, and I can enjoy you enjoying your animals and pets; however, this isn't in my DNA! The Lord made no mistake when He made me Mrs. Weeks and not Mrs. Noah! Had I been Mrs. Noah, I would not have survived the Mt. Ararat Cruise!

I would never be cruel to animals; I just don't care to be around them. However, whenever I am near animals, especially dogs, they either try to get in my lap or lay at my feet, where I immediately become frozen with fear of moving, for fear they may bite me! Seriously, I can be in a room full of people and one dog, and the dog will find me and sit at my feet or jump in my lap! (Yes, this has happened on more than one occasion!)

Even though I am not an animal lover, I appreciate your affection and love for your pets. So many of my friends have pets. I had one dear friend who lived alone; her pet of choice was a cat, my least favorite animal in the animal kingdom.

Her cat was her buddy; some days, the cat was the only one she had to talk to, so when her cat died suddenly, she was very distraught. When I heard the news about her cat's death and how upset she was, I immediately went to see her.

As I was driving over to her house, I was praying and asking the Lord to help me comfort her; I mean, honestly, I had no clue how to help my friend over the loss of her cat; I reminded the Lord that a cat was my least favorite of the animal kingdom! I also reminded the Lord that I was allergic to cats, so I asked Him to please hold back any sneezing fit that may develop from cat dander and please don't let my eyes swell shut; after all, I needed to drive back home.

As I was pleading my case to the Lord, I asked for wisdom and a large dose of compassion for a cat to comfort my friend. I asked Him, "How can I help her, Lord, when I don't like animals, especially cats?"

Then the Lord spoke to me in that still, small voice we all hear and said, *"Putter, grief is grief; it doesn't matter what a person is grieving over; the pain is the same. Remember how you felt when you lost your parents, and all you wanted to do was talk about them, and everyone changed the conversation?"*

I told the Lord, yes, I remembered that, and reminded Him that we were talking about a cat, not a person, and I was going to need His help!

So, here I am driving down the Interstate, giving myself a pep talk, "You can do this, Putter. Her grief is as traumatic as your grief was over Mom and Dad's passing; remember, grief is grief, and you cannot put any other label on it; it *is grief*! So, ask her about the cat and let her talk about him!

When I got to her house, as I hugged her, she cried for a few minutes, and then I asked her, "Tell me all about him; how long did you have him; how old was he when you got him?" I stayed a few more hours with her, and she talked about her pet and told me all the crazy things he did and the conversations she would have with him, and all the crazy quarks the cat had and honestly, by the time I left, I was sorry I never got to meet her pet, I think he would have been one "cool cat!"

Death is not the only situation in that I went from weeping to laughing. It happened many times during our years on the foreign mission field. Most of the adjusting in a foreign country can occur in four areas: food, culture, language, and money.

We had no problem with the food. Austrian and German foods were delicious, especially the bread and butter. I told a visitor once that if he ever heard that the Weeks family was down to bread and butter, please don't feel sorry for us. Yes, it was that delicious, but the coffee did take a little longer to get used to! The first cup I had, I looked at Dave and almost cried as I said, "How will I survive here with this coffee?" It tasted so strong, but a few weeks later, I had to laugh as I found myself asking for a refill!

The first cultural difference we encountered was farm living! I was used to farm country for part of my childhood was in the country, but Pennsylvania and Austrian country living are different! In Pennsylvania, the farmers kept their animals on their land and in fenced-off areas. In Austria, the farmers' house and barn were in the village, and early in the morning, they moved their cows up to the hillsides to graze for the day, and in late afternoon they moved them back down into the barns.

I have already told you about my fear of animals, so imagine my horror the day I decided to walk into our village with our younger kids when suddenly, I heard bells clanging and cows surrounding us! Yes, a herd of cows.

I was more frightened than the kids. Everything was an adventure of a lifetime to them, but I thought our lives were about to end! Imagine this "petrified of animals" person with her young children surrounded by cows, curious, big, dirty, smelly, drooling cows. Here I am, trying to tell my children that the cows were friendly and just came to say hello and welcome us to the neighborhood!

The only good thing was that this time, in my fear, I could actually talk! But inside, I was getting ready to panic and cry, and then I thought of something that made me laugh: I thought I didn't remember any scenes like this from *The Sound of Music*; for some reason, I began to laugh as the opening scene began to play through my head, you know where Julie Andrews comes over the hill and sings, "The hills are alive with the sound of music!" as she is carrying and clanging Cow Bells!

Once I laughed about that scene, for some reason, I wasn't frightened anymore! I guess *I just thought of a few of my favorite things, and then I didn't feel so bad!* (Sorry about that, I got carried away and could not help myself!)

The language learning phase is a very stressful time for any missionary. Our kids picked it up quickly; one night, we invited one of Dave's language teachers to have dinner with us, and when he arrived at our place, he saw our kids and the neighborhood kids outside playing, so he decided to figure out which were ours. When we called the kids in for dinner and introduced them to him, he was shocked at meeting them because they were not the children he thought were ours. He said their German had no American accent, and they spoke it perfectly! (I immediately began to pray for a childlike mind!)

Yes, our kids picked up the language fast; however, Mom and Dad took longer. Learning German was the most trying time of our first term on the field for me. It really can get to you if you do not have a sense of humor. So many times, as the proverbial phrase goes: "what I wanted to say got wrapped around my eye tooth, and I could not see what I was saying." But we had to learn it; there was no quick way to learn it. We would not learn it by osmosis; unfortunately, there was only one way to learn: Language School and a lot of midnight oil and hard studying!

The first year of language found me more in tears and frustration than it did in actual conversation. I had more on my plate than I could physically and mentally handle. By now, culture shock had set in with me, and Language School was five days a week and about 35 hours a week with around 5 hours of homework a night.

All six children were still with us, and our two older daughters cared for our little ones as they did their American homeschooling classes during my absence. The girls also helped the two younger ones with their American K-4 and K-5 studies.

Just letting the kids alone that long without either of us at home during the day took its toll on me as a mother. When I would get home at night, I would check on their school work, get supper ready, take care of whatever needed finishing around the house, and then hit the books myself. There were many nights and days that I just cried. I was torn between taking care of my kids and home and preparing to help Dave serve the Lord in starting a church. Finally, I had to admit I was not *Wonder Woman* and had to let something go.

I decided I was first and foremost a wife and mother, then a language student, so I dropped out of language school. Of course, this decision led to a guilt complex, but finally, through many tears and prayers, the Lord gave me peace about my decision, and I was back to being a wife and mom again.

The last year before our furlough, Dave finished all his language studies. So, he informed me that I was going back to language school, only this time he would be Mr. Mom and chief cook and bottle washer and do the laundry, and I would devote all my time to learning the language. He asked me if I would agree to one thing: would I still iron his shirts? He did not entirely trust the girls with it, and he did not like doing it. I told him I would be glad to do that for him.

Yes, this was a time of weeping for me, but there came a day when I could finally enjoy the laughing part. I will never forget this day! I was sitting on a park bench, waiting for Dave to come out of the post office, when a sweet elderly couple sat beside me and began speaking German with me. After about three sentences, they realized I was a foreigner and asked where I was from. The man did not believe it when I told them I was from the USA. He told me I was from England, and I replied, no, I was from the USA. Then he said again that he did not believe me, to which his wife got upset and told him that I should know where I was from, and he still insisted on me being from England because I did not speak German like an American!

Now that made me laugh out loud! I walked away thinking of another movie scene from *My Fair Lady* when Eliza Doolittle finally gets it, and Professor Higgins begins to sing, "She's Got It!"! Yep, I walked away that day singing: "I got it, by George, I've got it!"

Another weeping turned to laughter situation that we had no control over was money, or I should say the lack of it! However, through the years, the Lord has taught me that He not only owns the cattle on a thousand hills but the hills as well, and my favorite biblical phrase is *Jehovah-jireh; the Lord will provide,* and He sure did during our first term on the foreign mission field.

When we arrived in Austria, the value of the American dollar was good, and we had enough monthly support for a family of eight and the higher prices of the European economy. However, after a few months, the value of the American dollar dropped in half. To give you an idea of what this meant, our $440.00 monthly rent for our house now costs us $880.00. Our expenses had now doubled, but our monthly income remained the same! To make things more nerve-racking, we were now in the process of moving to Germany to go to language school, another added expense that had now doubled in price.

Many missionaries were packing up and returning to the States to raise more support; one missionary said he slept like a baby; he woke up every two hours and cried! During this time, we knew we needed to trust the Lord for everything; this is when praying for the Lord to give us our daily bread had meaning to it.

Dave and I agreed that as long as the Lord provided for us, we would stay until our scheduled furlough when we would return to the States and raise more support to cover our loss. I will be honest with you there were times when I just wanted to sit down and weep, but then the Lord would supply a need we had through many interesting ways; for instance, a phone call from a friend who said, The Lord put us on his heart, and he knew that we had a need, and he wanted to know what it was and how he could help!

Another way He provided was through another missionary serving in a country where the US dollar was strong. He sent us a monthly offering until we came home on furlough to raise more support. Another young man, who had been in Dave's Sunday School class he taught before going to Bible College, had graduated from high school and had a well-paying job. This young man sent money to our account until we could be on furlough. Several churches we had never been in during deputation began to support us monthly. His provisions for us were unending!

Yes, what started as a weeping time ended in a joyous celebration because we could stay and finish language school only because He controlled our situation and not us!

This time I think God laughed; when He heard us say, "As long as He provides, we will stay!" I could imagine Him saying to Gabriel and Michael, "This is going to be good!" And, it was, we never missed paying a bill nor went hungry; He supplied all our needs, and we were able to stay, learn the language and return home on our scheduled furlough. I know this is terrible English, but it sure is terrific Theology . . . Ain't God good?

Bettenell Huntznicke said, *"Laughter is God's hand on the shoulder of a troubled world."* Yes, there are times that we will have absolutely no control over the situations in our life, and our world will be troubled and our grief overwhelming, and it will be a time of weeping, but keep on looking for the time of laughing, for it will come, when you need it the most!

Dear Lord Jesus,
Thank You for those times of weeping that only You can turn into laughter. May we always be mindful of You walking with us, and may we always be a shining light for You in difficult times. Even in our grief, may we point people to You. And when our weeping turns to laughing, may we always remember Your love, kindness, and grace showed to us during those weeping times of life, and may we always be mindful to help others in their time of weeping so they can soon smile awhile.

Getting older happens to all of us! Sooner or later, you will have to admit; you aren't as young as you used to be. The aging process will suddenly be breathing down your neck, and you will wonder when and how this happened. However, one day, you will realize what Kitty O'Neill Collins said is true, *"Aging seems to be the only available way to live a long life."*

I must admit that the older I get, the more I find myself laughing at, the older I get! But I wasn't always that way; in fact, the idea of growing old used to bother me. I understood that aging was a part of life, but I would allow my overactive imagination to think of crazy scenarios about getting older. I would think about illnesses that would leave me dependent on others or in a vegetative state and being fed intravenously for the rest of my days!

What helped me come out of this mindset was meeting many incredible saintly older men and women who happily anticipated their Homegoing and meeting the Lord face to face.

What a joy and blessing these older folks were to me.

I will be forever grateful to Granny Smith and Ruth Chappell. These precious ladies were examples of growing old gracefully. Each was looking forward to the joy and anticipation of the next life when they would be with the Lord in a place where we will never grow old, and until then, they were enjoying each day of the journey Home.

Granny Smith had a favorite poem she loved to recite: it was:

> *Yesterday He helped me,*
> *Today He did the same*
> *How long will this continue?*
> *Forever, praise His name!*

She knew that "forever" meant forever, and even in old age, He would continue to help her; even to Glory, He would be with her!

These two precious ladies helped me overcome my fearful thoughts of old age and showed me how to enjoy life in old age was to trust in the Lord and be thankful for all His blessings, even all the problems that come with old age. ***Getting older to them was not an age, but an attitude!***

And they had the best attitude about getting older, and I wanted what they had.

These two extraordinary ladies truly understood and lived out Ps 37:25: *I have been young, and now am old; yet have I not seen the righteous forsaken, nor his seed begging bread.* They continued to praise the Lord and enjoy life right up to the time He called them home to be with Him.

They were living examples of growing old gracefully and having fun in the process! After meeting these precious women of God, I was no longer fearful of getting old or the aging process.

Yes, we all face old age; it doesn't happen overnight. It begins with our first breath of air! Theodore Roosevelt said: *"Old age is like everything else. To make a success of it, you've got to start young."* And so it is, the very day we are born, we begin to age.

Have you ever thought of what a baby learns and how they change in the first year of their life? They go from an infant to a toddler to walking, and then they are driving a car in the blink of an eye! Yes, we change from a tiny infant completely dependent on someone to care for our every need to a little girl running through the fields holding butterflies to a budding young woman lying in bed holding the heating pad!

Then before you know it, you are a young wife, and your body is changing again and expanding to bring a beautiful bundle of unorganized opportunities into the world! And just by the time all your bundles of opportunities are grown up and on their own and you have finally adjusted to your empty nest, you find yourself doing a Google search for **cures for hot flashes**!

I like how the Bible describes this time in a woman's life. In 1Cor 7:36, this phrase is used *"she pass the flower of her age."* Strong's Concordance says this phrase means: Beyond the bloom of life. How poetic is that? However, Strong's continues with this: over ripe, plump, and ripe. Then he adds: and so is a greater danger of defilement! *Isn't that just precious?* I think this may be a nice Ancient Greek way of saying: she gets fat, miserable, and a bit psychotic!

Yes, ladies, our bodies are in a constant state of change. Whether we like it or not, we all must come to grips with the thought that we are fearfully and wonderfully made. We all go through the most significant change in our lives; menopause; however, I must admit, my journey through menopause was more fearful than wonderful!

Did you know this medical fact about menopause? It begins around age 40 and can take up to ten years; the first few years are referred to as perimenopause. I looked up the meaning of the prefix *peri,* and one meaning was: the word "near." I first thought of an exit sign indicating you are near your exit. When you see the exit sign, the first thing you do is slow down. I guess this perimenopausal time helps us adjust to the changes *slowly* by seeing and experiencing one small thing at a time, like waking up one morning and seeing chin hairs!

I mean, really, overnight, CHIN HAIRS are there! And wait until you try pulling them out; I am convinced they are cemented in! Now I know we women came from a man's rib, but honestly, I was not prepared to share facial hair with him! But I guess if we get to share men's facial hair, it is only fair then that they must share in the menopausal time of our life. Sounds reasonable to me, don't you think so?

The next change I noticed was sleep disturbances; either I slept well or didn't sleep at all. I also began to snore at night when I did sleep! I would wake myself up from snoring, thinking it was Dave snoring! Then came the night sweats! Just wait, ladies, those of you who are always cold at night, one day you will be throwing off the covers at night and sweating like a boxer in a ring during the big match! I wonder how many of you older women have stood before the open freezer to get cool, or am I the only one?

Also, during menopause, I found that there is something about the honesty of a child that makes you want to cover their mouth with duct tape in public, especially when they think it necessary to inform you how your neck is getting red and continuing the *"breaking news: announcement"* as you turn red from the neck to your face to the top of your head, while sitting in a waiting room at the doctor's office.

I must admit, that is the one thing I miss about menopause, being hot! Old age has turned off my internal thermostat, and now I always stay cold. So many times, I wish I would not have complained about those hot flashes, for I could use some "body heat" today.

What I did not expect was crying spells! For no reason, the floodgates would open, and I could not hold back the tears! I would pray and ask the Lord to let me hold it together until the kids went to bed. Often, I would hop in the shower to cry, and if the kids noticed my eyes were red, I would tell them I got soap in my eyes!

Once, I walked into Church on a Sunday morning, and someone complimented me on how nice I looked! For some unknown mystical reason, that made me cry! I went to the lady's room, locked the door, and cried until I could compose myself!

The worse part was that I could not take the hormone replacement medicine that doctors give us "mature women" to help with all the problems that come with this time of life. The side effects from these meds were worse than the problem I was taking them for; one major side effect was leg cramps! I would be walking, and suddenly, the calf of my leg would cramp, and my leg would not straighten out! (Perhaps that is what happened when I tried to go through the kitchen window!)

Headaches were also a problem with these meds. So, I finally stopped taking them; I figured if I survived menopause, I would succumb to some cancer caused by the medications meant to ease the effects of menopause!

I got to where I barely liked myself, and I could not imagine how my family put up with me! Then, finally, I found something that helped me; even though my doctor told me I was scraping the bottom of the barrel with my newfound medicine; however, if it helped, I should use it.

What I found was a cream made from an extract from sweet potatoes! Now, I was not only a "hot" but a "sweet" potato, but it worked so well that Dave called it my "happy cream." I never knew how difficult this time was for Dave until I was finally myself again; that is when he told me that if I should die first, he wanted me to know that he would never remarry a younger woman. I told him that I would not have any objection to him remarrying if I should die first, then he said, "Honey, you did not hear what I said. I said I would not marry a YOUNGER woman! I lived through one menopausal woman; I am not doing that again!" Bless his heart!

Yes, Ladies, we are fearfully and wonderfully made, although the only thing I found fearful and wonderful during those years of menopause was that my family still loved me after it passed.

But ladies, one important blessing about menopause was that I no longer had to worry about another round of baby bottles and diapers after it passed! So, see, there is a silver lining in every cloud!

Once I got through it, I thought life would be a breeze then; before I knew it, I was facing *the life of the elderly*, and boy, is this one a hoot!

See, menopause was just a forerunner to old age, and if you can laugh through menopause, Honey, you are in for the time of your life and some terrific laughs. Old age is entertainment at its finest! You will know when you have reached this stage of life when your grandchildren tell you, "Oh, Mamaw, you're so cute!"

I don't mind getting older; after all, the senior discounts are terrific; I just didn't expect it to be so soon! I mean, like overnight, it arrived! I would have taken better care of myself if I had known it was coming this soon!

The first thing I noticed was that everyone in my family began to mumble when they spoke to me, but at one point. I realized they may have been right; perhaps, it was my hearing and not them mumbling. One day, my granddaughter, Brooke, was in our bathroom and kept asking me if I had something she needed; after asking for the third time and not hearing her clearly, I went to the bathroom and asked her why she wanted mushrooms in the bathroom. She had asked for a hairbrush! Yes, old age is very entertaining!

Then there are the trifocal lenses in my eyeglasses! A word of advice, if you need trifocals, DO NOT attempt to go on the escalator when you first wear them, leaving the eye doctor's office! Remember, Ladies, a word to the wise is sufficient!

One day I noticed I wasn't moving as fast as I used to, but I figured out why: you see, by the time I got up and started to walk, I forgot where I was going and why I was going there, so I walked slower hoping to remember where and why I was going there!

When I was younger, I wondered why older people shuffle when walking! Well, now I know why. If I pick up my feet, I may lose my balance or trip over something, so I do the "70's shuffle."

In the morning, just getting out of bed takes longer. First, I throw my legs over the edge, sit straight up for a few seconds, and slowly rise to my feet, you know, for the blood to flow to the top of my head slowly.

It does take me a little longer to get ready because I need to do more than just "put on my face." First, I need to find my glasses, and since I am now in trifocals, I need to make sure they are on my face just right, or I see double, then I find the hearing aids and get the right one in the right ear, this is another reason why I always put the glasses on first! Then I head to the bathroom to get my partial teeth in! By now, I am feeling productive!

Even my vocabulary changed, "taking a spin" means something entirely different to me now, and I can take a spin by just getting up too fast! One positive thing is that my calendar is always full. I am always making visits; there is a visit to the cardiologist, pulmonologist, optometrist, Primary Care doctor, Vascular Surgeon, dentist, and dermatologist.

I walk a lot more than when I was younger; you would be surprised how many places one can put a cell phone and how long it takes to find it! It is like playing the game *Clue*, but instead of Who Did It, it's Where Is It!

I have heard that the longer a couple is together, the more they begin to look like each other. I didn't mind my hair turning gray like Dave's, but when it started turning loose like his, I was concerned that this might be true and was about to do a Google search for a good wig maker! But my niece (my hairstylist) found a shampoo and conditioner that is helping to make my hair thicker. But there are only so many ways to comb your bangs over to cover up the bald spots!

The one thing that blindsided me, really blindsided me, was the Macular Degeneration of my right eye. With macular degeneration, I am losing the central vision of the right eye, and everything I see with that eye is distorted and wavy, and anything I look at with that eye has a cloudy dark spot in the middle. It is like looking in a funhouse mirror with a blurry center and smudged marks on it!

With this eye problem, my perception is off. For example, I was putting toothpaste on my toothbrush, or so I thought. As I squeezed the tube of toothpaste, I thought it would go on the brush, but it shot across the sink. I have learned to put the toothpaste tube on the brush before squeezing the tube.

Threading a needle is fun! The thread goes to the back or to the front and sometimes above the needle. The sewing machine needle is the most fun to thread between the trifocals and the Macular problem; it is very difficult. One day I tried to use a needle threader, but that didn't work, so I used the next best thing, my cell phone! Yes, it worked great, I called Mary Beth, and she came and re-threaded it for me and finished what I was sewing!

One evening at a restaurant, I tried to put my straw into a rather large glass; I felt like I was playing *Whack a Mole*! Another night I was putting on nail polish; I put it on the table, on my fingers, and a bit on my nails. Fortunately, it was clear polish!

Putting make-up on is another entertaining pastime, especially my eyebrows. The right one is no problem, but the left one is always a bit; well, let's say my eyebrows are never the same.

There have been times I have put on two different earrings or a piece of clothing was put on inside out. But it is okay when someone says something to me; I tell them I am experimenting to see how many people are observant and notice things and will say something to me. (At least that is my story, and I am sticking with it!)

However, I found my silver lining in this "cloud" of Macular Degeneration, actually two silver linings: I still have one good eye, and I only see half the dust in the house. Isn't God good? All the time, He is good!

Not only have I learned to laugh about growing old, but I have learned that this is a time of wonder. I wonder where I put my house keys; I wonder where my purse is; I wonder did I take my vitamins, but most of all, I wonder, in all these years, what has getting older taught me?

So here are a few things I've learned from getting older:

Getting older has taught me to appreciate old age, for it is a privilege that some have never experienced. (My Daddy was buried on his 44th birthday!)

Getting older has taught me to be kinder and gentler to others.

Getting older has taught me the pleasure of refusing to eat spinach and Brussels sprouts without being denied dessert.

Getting older has taught me that some things aren't worth fighting over.

Getting older has taught me what things are worth fighting over.

Getting older has taught me it is okay to forget some things, for some things aren't worth remembering.

Getting older has taught me there will be times when my heart is broken, but that is a good thing, for how else would I have experienced the joy of a mended heart?

Getting older has taught me that my hearing will go bad, but that's okay, for some things aren't worth hearing.

Getting older has taught me that old age does not have a monopoly on wisdom.

Getting older has taught me that there will be days of aches and pains, but that is okay, for I can still enjoy the sunrise and the sunset and children playing and enjoying the day.

Getting older has taught me that there will be days of plenty and days of leanness, but He will continue to supply my needs and throw in a few wants along this journey of life.

Getting older has taught me that laughter really is the best medicine.

Getting older has taught me that good memories and friends are worth keeping.

Getting older has taught me that Mom was right; some people grow up, and others just grow old!

Getting older has taught me that a day around children of any age is a good day.

Getting older has taught me that what people think of me is not important.

Getting older has taught me that what people think of my Lord is important.

Getting older has taught me that I have had a very blessed life and am getting closer to a land where we will never grow old!

So, come my friends, grow old with me; the best is yet to be!

Dear Lord Jesus,
Thank You for the experience of old age. May You be honored and glorified through the process. May we grow old gracefully with wisdom, mercy, grace, and love as we draw others to You, and whether young or old, may we be a light for You, and may we always find something in old age that will make us smile awhile.

When God Laughs

I found this great quote from a very well-known doctor; I am sure you will recognize his name:

From there to here, from here to there,
funny things are everywhere.
Dr. Seuss

Yes, funny things are everywhere, and laughter is a normal human response. The Bible teaches that laughter is good, like medicine for us, and we can safely say that a laugh a day keeps the doctor away, but have you ever considered when God laughs and what makes God laugh?

God does laugh; the Bible tells us God laughs, and I am sure when He sees some of the predicaments; I get myself into, He laughs and calls Michael and Gabriel and says, "Hey guys come over here. You aren't going to believe what she has got herself into now!"

Yes, God laughs; we read in Ps 37:12-13: The wicked plotteth against the just, and gnasheth upon him with his teeth. The Lord shall laugh at him: for he seeth that his day is coming.

Here we have an account of the wicked planning and doing wicked things against God's people, but in verse 13, He laughs at them; why? Because He knows their end!

In Ps 2:1-4, we read where God laughs at those against Him: Why do the heathen rage, and the people imagine a vain thing? The kings of the earth set themselves, and the rulers take counsel together, against the LORD, and his anointed, saying, Let us break their bands asunder, and cast away their cords from us. He that sitteth in the heavens shall laugh: the Lord shall have them in derision.

They are making plans, BUT He has His plan. How foolish of them to think they can conquer His people and ultimately Him. Yes, God laughs at their plans. And I am sure He laughs at ours.

In the movie *Fiddler on the Roof*, Tevye, the father, laments that he is a poor farmer and has a question he presents to the Lord in a song: *If I Were a Rich Man*. He asks the Lord if he had been a wealthy man, would it have changed some vast eternal plan? It is a catchy song and a very good illustration of how people still question the Lord's plan for their lives.

There is much truth in an old Yiddish saying: *"Man plans, and God laughs!"*

Like every young married couple, Dave and I had our plans, and, I am sure, God laughed! To begin with, as a young girl, I always said I would never marry a preacher, and when I met someone, I wanted to find a man who had the same plans that I had. Fortunately, when I met Dave, we both had the same plans.

I wanted to marry a man who knew how to work and provide for his family, a man who would allow me to be a stay-at-home Mom and care for our children. Dave wanted a wife willing to be a stay-at-home wife willing to take care of his home and children, and we both wanted someone to grow old with together! Dave and I had a solid plan. Our plan was for him to work his way up the corporate ladder, and eventually, we would own a horse farm on a beautiful country estate and only have two children.

Yes, only two children, for we were going to do our part for the population explosion theory going around in the late 1960s, and from Nov 1966 to Dec 1972, we were on track to achieving our plan. We had our two children; Dave was on the 2nd rung of the corporate ladder; we were one acre into our country estate and had one horse and one pony of our horse stock! We had a solid plan and a good life, and we enjoyed every minute of it, and I'm sure God laughed!

You know the Lord can use anything He wants to get our attention, and, in our case, he used one of the very things we were working so hard for and building our life around, a horse! Yes, a horse! Dave had bought a horse from a horse auction, and it had a habit of rearing up and throwing off its rider. When Dave was younger, he trained horses, and he knew what to do to break the horse. We just knew that this horse would soon be eating out of Dave's hand and obeying every command of his master; I am sure God was laughing by now!

During one of the training sessions, the horse not only reared up but flipped over on its back; unfortunately (humanly speaking), Dave was still in the saddle when the horse flipped on its back; and Dave was pinned underneath the horse and the saddle. So, when the horse rolled to get back up, the saddle horn snapped Dave's femur bone, and the bone splintered into small fragments.

A few days later, the doctor told Dave he was very fortunate that none of the splintered bone fragments punctured the artery in his leg; had that happened, he would have probably bled to death before the ambulance arrived. Dave began to think about death, and the thought went through his mind, how could he have peace with God?

God had gotten Dave's attention, and Dave wasn't laughing!

During Dave's months of recovery, the Lord had our attention. At this time, I began taking our two little girls to the church with our neighbors, They invited us to come to church with them the first week we moved into our home, but I made some lame excuse as to why we could not go that Sunday and went inside and said to Dave, "Just our luck, we moved next to Holy Rollers! They go to church three times a week, twice on Sunday and Wednesday night!" I think back to that statement now, and I can imagine God laughing and saying, "Just wait, Putter, one day, so will you."

After Dave's accident, the girls and I visited the church with them. I was amazed at what I heard and saw. I had never attended a church like this before; the people carried Bibles to Church, and the Pastor preached from the Bible. God now had my attention, and I wasn't laughing either!

After Dave could walk reasonably well on crutches and handle going up and down steps, he started going with us to Church and Sunday School. Long story short, in 1973, Dave admitted that he was a sinner, confessed his sins, asked the Lord to forgive him and gave his life to Jesus Christ, and committed his life to follow the Lord's leadership; however, it took me a bit longer.

As I watched Dave grow in the Lord, I knew I wanted what he had, and I made a profession of faith, but I never really admitted that I was a sinner and needed a Savior! So, for over two years, I was one miserable person headed to hell with a heavenly hope!

I was finding it harder and harder to act like a Christian. You can only "fake" it for so long! Without the Holy Spirit's aid in one's life, it is impossible to be like Christ. However, it is the will of God that all should come to repentance and salvation. The Lord did not have to break my leg, but He did have to break through my pride and self-righteousness. I am sure this did not take the Lord by surprise, even though it did me.

As I was growing up, I was always told what a good little girl I was, and I heard more than once how good of a teenager I was, and by the time I grew up, I was convinced I really was *Miss Goody Two Shoes*; because *when you hear something enough times, good or bad, you begin to believe it*!

It wasn't until I came face to face with the truth of Isa 64:6 that I saw myself as God saw me!

Isa 64:6 But we are all as an unclean thing, and all our righteousnesses (all my goodness) are as filthy rags; and we all do fade as a leaf; and our iniquities, like the wind, have taken us away.

On December 28, 1975, I admitted to the Lord; that I was not as good as I thought; in fact, I was a sinner, and I confessed that fact to the Lord and asked Him to forgive me and save me. So finally, Dave and I were on the Lord's path for our lives.

In 1980 we completely surrendered to God's plan for our life. We sold our home, gave away the horses, packed up a U-haul, and with our now four little girls in the car, we headed to

Greenville, SC, to finally start on God's plan for our lives, and we have never missed anything we left behind!

There was nothing wrong with our plan, we could have served God with it, but it wasn't His plan. We had a good plan, but God had a better plan for us! He has moved us from PA to SC to Germany and Austria to GA! His plan has been the BEST plan; actually, His plan has been a BLESSED plan for us.

While Dave started Bible College, I prepared to be a Pastor's wife. I just thought that was where we were headed; I even had the type of Church we would serve in; we would probably be back in PA, and Dave would pastor a small country church with about 100 people, so imagine my surprise when Dave came home one night and told me the Lord was dealing with him about Missions, and Dave was thinking about Australia!

Australia! I was still trying to adjust to being away from PA!

Then I met some wonderful Missionary wives, and I went into a spiral of overactive imaginations that were taking hold of my thinking! Each of these ladies could sing like a nightingale or play some instrument beautifully; they were graceful and could speak elegantly without turning red from the neck up. The more I was around them, the worse I felt.

I kept thinking, "Lord, I know You make no mistakes, so maybe Dave did; I mean, missionary and in a foreign country! And Lord, I can't even carry a tune in a basket, let alone sing a song and speak to a crowd; oh Lord, I am not sure I can do this!"

Then I began to see myself trying to walk up to a platform to speak at a meeting, tripping up the steps and stammering as I tried to speak to ladies!

I then started having nightmares about us moving to Australia. I would have the same dream repeatedly. I would dream that I was hanging clothes on wash-lines outside and Mary Beth, about ten months old, was playing on the grass by my feet. While she was playing, a kangaroo would come hopping out of the woods, pick her up, put her in its pouch, and run off with her into the woods! These thoughts and nightmares went on for some months.

We continued praying for direction from the Lord when, after much prayer, Dave knew beyond a shadow of a doubt that the Lord was calling us to Austria! For some reason, I was so relieved when he told me it was Austria where we would be, for my kangaroo nightmare had finally ended.

However, now my poor mother was the one whose overactive imagination was running wild about us going to a foreign land; bless her heart; we could not convince Mom that Austria was not a communist country! She just knew we would be arrested and put in jail, and the kids would be in a government-run orphanage.

We kept trying to tell her that Austria was a freedom of religion country, and we would not be thrown into jail and live on bread and water. Finally, one of my siblings told her she had nothing to worry about, for if they did throw us in jail, all Putter had to do was sing 24/7, and after a few days of listening to her, the Austrian government would pay the USA to take us back!

Mom's fears finally stopped, and although I could laugh at my sibling's advice, I started having nightmares again about Austria! By now, we had our son David, and Mary Beth was four, and in my new nightmare, they both were playing outside when out of the hills, a bear would come and take them both away!

I am so thankful for the Lord's patience and longsuffering with me during this time, for once my crazy nightmares stopped, I started having thoughts and doubts about where and how I fit into this ministry in missions. I could not see where my place was. I was not like the other missionary wives I met. I was neither musically talented nor had any exceptional talents to offer the churches or the Austrian people. I was just me, a wife and mother, married to a passionate preacher with whom I wanted to share this ministry life, but I did not know how I fit into this plan.

Finally, everything came together for me, and I received my answer from the Lord, but I had to get to Austria to receive it! The Lord gave me the answer to all my fears and questions one day in our kitchen in Austria!

I was showing one of the young girls in our neighborhood how to make peanut brittle, and she was so excited about learning how to make it; as I looked at her face and watched her excitement, the Lord spoke to me and said, "Do you think she wants to hear you sing, Putter?"

In that instant, I realized that when the Lord called Dave into missions, I was me, Putter, wife, and mother. Therefore, He could use me, just as I am, despite my insecurities, off-key singing, and fumbling speech; after all, if the Lord used a donkey to speak to a prophet, He can use me to speak to others, no matter what country I am in!

The fact is, He used the German language to prove to me that He still uses donkeys today for His honor and glory. While in Austria, I could not understand why everyone called Dave by his name and the kids by their names, but I was always Frau Weeks. I knew they did not use my nickname Putter because nicknames were for family and only very close friends, but then the Lord allowed me to find out why I was always Frau Weeks.

When a German-speaking person tries to pronounce my name Ethel, they pronounce the "th" like "s" and pronounce Ethel, *Esel,* which would have been fine with me; after all, I realized I did not pronounce their names perfectly either. Then I found out that *Esel* is the German word for a donkey!

They would not say my name because they did not want to offend me, but what a lesson this was for me and one I needed to know that today, God can still use a donkey for His honor and glory! I am living proof!

Dear Lord,
Thank You for the plans You have for each of us, all different plans for our individual lives, but all for Your honor and Glory!

Lord, When our plans make You laugh, may we always be willing to follow Your plans for our lives, for Your plans are always the BEST and the most BLESSED plans for us!

Most importantly, Lord, may we never forget each day to take the time to:
smile awhile and give our face a rest, and raise our hands to the One we love the best, and smile awhile!

Dear Friend

Thank you for reading this book; I trust it brought a smile to your face and brightened your day. I pray for each of you who may read it that you will find something to smile about in each phase of your life. May the Lord bless each of you daily with His abundant joy and presence.

Below are a few verses that have helped me when I found it difficult for a while to smile. I trust they will encourage your heart as well.

Fear:
Ps 56:3-4; Ps 56:11; Ps 23:4; Ps 34:4; Ps 27:1

Uncontrollable Situations:
Jos 1:9; John 14:27; Ps 46:1; Mt 5:4; 1 Pt 5:7; Ps 55:22

Old Age:
Ps 37:25; Ps 71:18; Ps 92:14; Isa 46:4

God's Plans:
Mic 6:8; Jer 29:11; Pr 3:5-6; Ps 16:11

As each new day dawns on your journey through life, always remember to smile awhile and raise your hand to the One you love the best! He is worthy.

God bless you, my Friend,

"Putter"

www.ingramcontent.com/pod-product-compliance
Lightning Source LLC
Chambersburg PA
CBHW060419050426
42449CB00009B/2027